Contents

SCHOOL FROM ABOVE

Why is a school like a map? At school you learn all sorts of useful things. Maps are useful too. They teach us about people and places.

Maps help you learn about the world around you, including at school.

What are maps?

Maps are drawings of the landscape from above. Imagine climbing to the top of a tall building and looking down. Houses, streets and trees look very different from this viewpoint. Maps show the landscape from this position, called an aerial view.

This photo of a school was taken from a plane.

This map shows the same school.

TRY THIS!

To make a map you have to learn to draw things from above. This can be hard at first, but gets easier with practice. Try making a map of objects on a desk or table, looking down from directly above.

A SCHOOL IN SYMBOLS

Maps don't show everything you can see from a tall building. That would make the map too complicated. Buildings are just shown as outlines. Maps use special signs called symbols to show important features. Symbols make the map clear and simple, so it is easy to read.

KEY

SCH	School
✝	Church
🌳	Wood
〰	Lake
═	Road

Drawing of a school in a village.

Map of the same school, with key.

Types of symbols

Map symbols can be letters, such as Sch for School. Or they can be very simple drawings. A drawing of a tree can mean a wood. Roads are shown as lines. Parks and playing fields are shown as coloured areas.

The key at the side explains what the symbols mean.

TRY THIS!

Maps use symbols instead of written labels. Copy the map below and use symbols instead of labels. Use symbols you know or make them up. Don't forget to add a key.

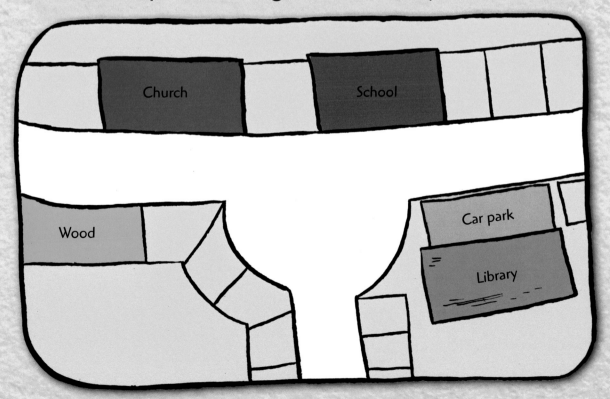

Church

School

Wood

Car park

Library

7

DIRECTIONS TO THE CLASSROOM

Maps show the location of buildings on a street, or classrooms in a school. The view from above helps you understand exactly where things are in relation to one another.

Maps help you find your way around a school with many classrooms, like this one.

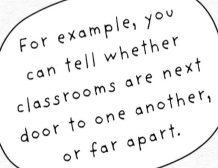

For example, you can tell whether classrooms are next door to one another, or far apart.

Finding the way

Maps can be used to find your way from one place to another. If you look at a map, you can tell whether to go left, right or straight on to reach the place you want to get to.

If there are several different ways, you can use the map to plan the best route.

KEY

☐ Door

⚊ Boys' toilet

⚊ Girls' toilet

Hall

Class 1

Class 4

Library

TRY THIS!

Look at the map above. Your friend in Class 1 wants to visit you in Class 4, but doesn't know how to get there. Can you write down the directions? Look at the map again. There are two possible routes, indoors and outdoors. Which is the quickest route?

PLAN OF A CLASSROOM

Builders follow the plan to construct the building.

Plans are maps that show a small area, such as a classroom, in a lot of detail. Architects use plans to design buildings. Everything is drawn and measured very carefully.

What do plan maps show?

Plan maps show features such as doors and windows. They may also show furniture such as tables and cupboards.

Teachers use a plan of the classroom to arrange the furniture, to make sure there is enough space for everyone.

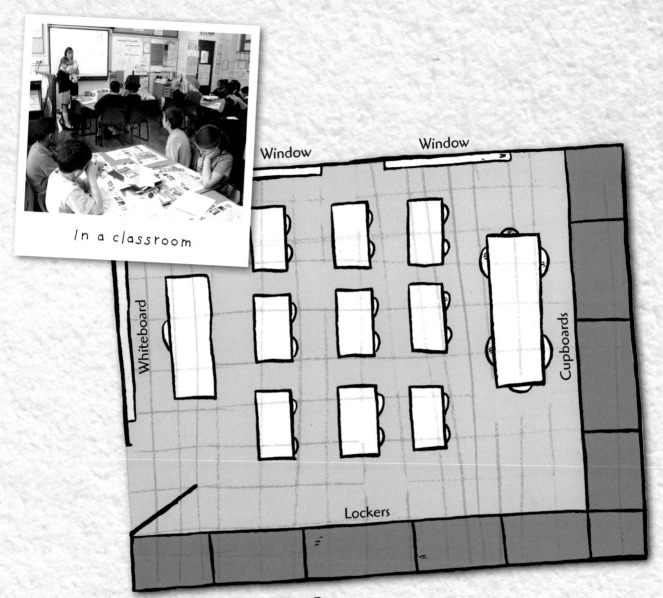

In a classroom

Window
Window
Whiteboard
Cupboards
Lockers

TRY THIS!

Make a plan of your classroom using your footsteps to measure distances. Count the number of steps it takes to walk from front to back, and then across the room. Draw the room on squared paper. Every square stands for one footstep. Count and measure tables and cupboards, and mark them on your map.

A SCHOOL TO DIFFERENT SCALES

A map that showed everything lifesize would be far too big to use! All maps show things smaller than lifesize, so they fit on a piece of paper.

Everything on the map is shrunk to the same size. This is called the scale. The scale used on the map is shown in a bar at the side.

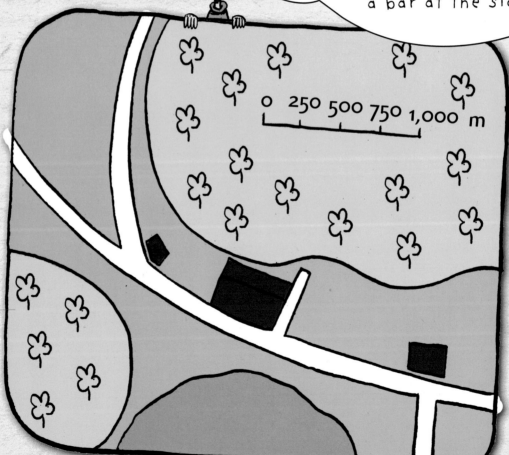

0 250 500 750 1,000 m

This small-scale map shows a school and its surroundings.

Different scales

Some maps show a small area, such as a school, in a lot of detail. Other maps show a larger area, such as a city, or even a whole country, but in less detail. Maps of different scales are useful in different ways.

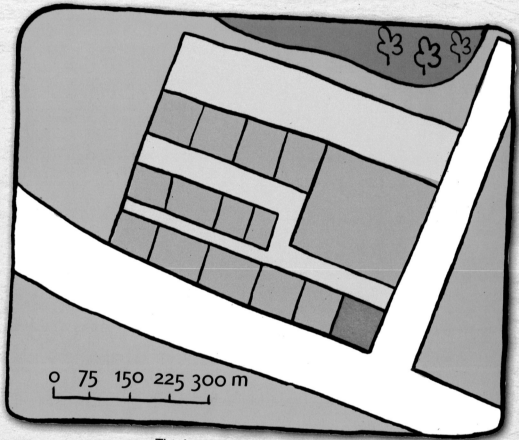

0 75 150 225 300 m

This large-scale map shows a school.

TRY THIS!

Compare the two maps shown on this page. Which map would you use to find your way from one classroom to another? Which map would you use to find your way to school?

USING SCALE IN THE HALL

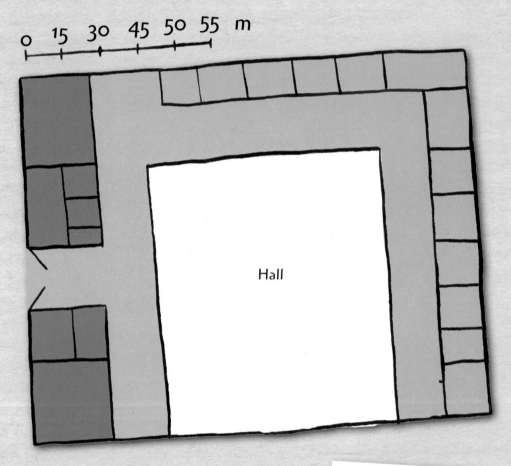

0 15 30 45 50 55 m

Hall

The hall is the largest building in the school. Everyone meets here for assembly. Knowing a map's scale can help you work out distances in a large space like this, either indoors or outdoors.

Bigger or smaller?

Always look at the map's scale. On small-scale maps that show a large area, every centimetre on the map may stand for 500 metres (0.5 km) on the ground. On large-scale maps, like the one below, 1 centimetre may stand for 100 metres (0.1 km).

Knowing the map's scale helps you work out how long it will take you to walk between two places shown on the map.

TRY THIS!

Make a map of your school hall by measuring the room in paces. Count the number of paces you take to cover the length and width of the hall. Decide on a scale, for example 1 cm for every pace. Make a map on a large piece of paper and mark the scale on the map.

COMPASS POINTS IN THE PLAYGROUND

In the playground, spin around and then look straight ahead. You are facing in a particular direction – either north, south, east or west, or somewhere in between.

North, south, east and west are the four main points of the compass. We use compass directions to locate places on a map or in real life.

A compass rose shows the four main compass points, arranged in a circle.

Using a compass

A compass is a useful tool that shows you which way you are facing or walking. The compass has a red magnetic needle that always points north. From that you can work out the other compass directions. Compass points are marked on many maps. North is usually at the top of the map.

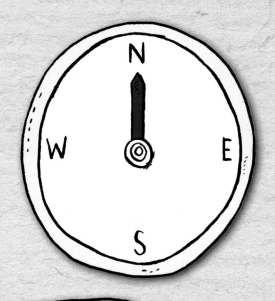

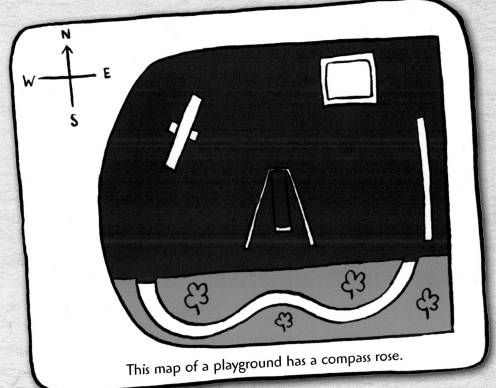

This map of a playground has a compass rose.

TRY THIS!

Find or make a map of your school playground. Check a compass to find out which way is north, and mark the four main compass points on the map.

MORE COMPASS WORK

The points of the compass can be used to locate places on a map in relation to one another. Look at the map below. The hall is north of the science block.

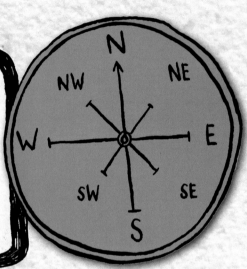

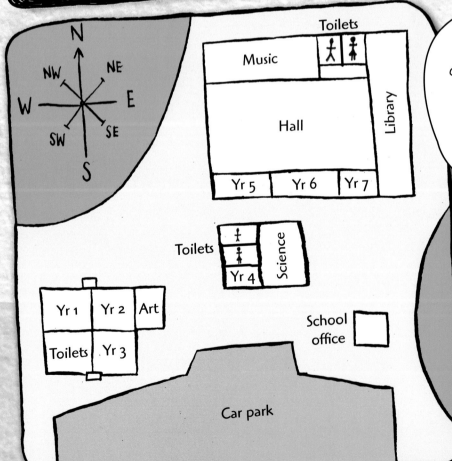

Compass directions can also help you find your way on a walk, for example in the school grounds.

The four main points of the compass are always arranged in the same way. Going clockwise from the top, they are north, east, south and west. Remember the order using this sentence: Naughty Elephants Squirt Water.

In between the four main compass points are four more points: northeast, southeast, southwest and northwest. These can help you pinpoint places exactly.

The school grounds are a great place to practise using a compass.

TRY THIS!

Look at the map and answer these questions:

- In which direction would you move to get from the hall to the science block?
- In which direction would you move to get from Year 6 classroom to the library?

LAND USE AT A SCHOOL

Some maps have extra information about what the land or buildings are used for. These are called land use maps.

On the map below, different colours are used to show private houses and public buildings, such as the school, library, police station and shops.

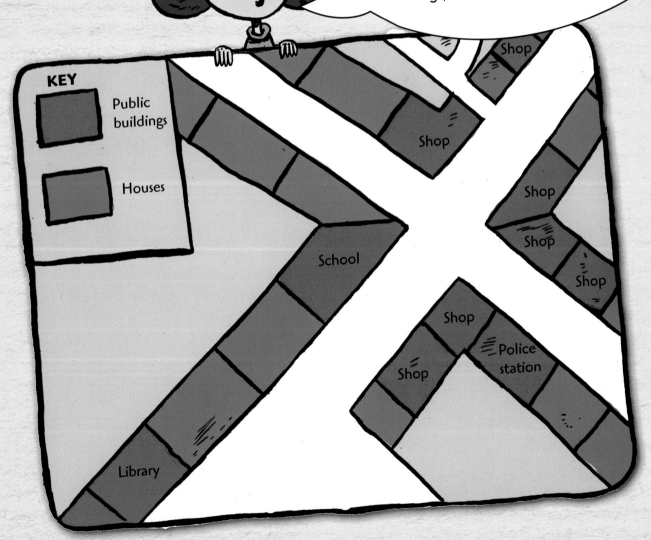

KEY

Public buildings

Houses

Shop

Shop

Shop

Shop

Shop

Shop

School

Shop

Police station

Library

What are rooms used for?

Land use maps are also used in schools. Rooms with different uses, such as classrooms, hall, staff room, and library are shown in different colours. The colours make it even easier to spot things on the map.

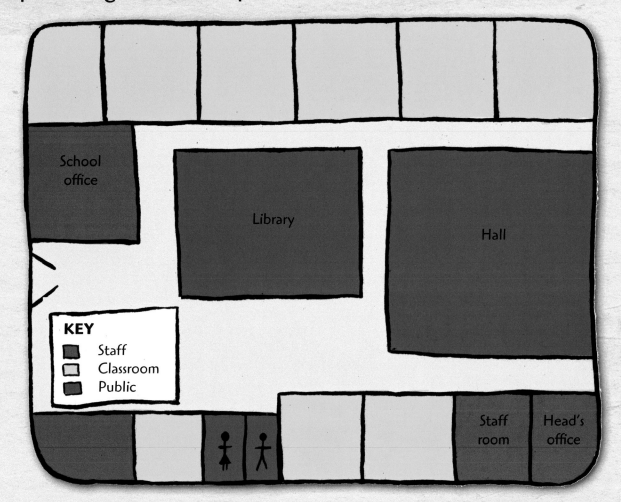

KEY
- Staff
- Classroom
- Public

School office

Library

Hall

Staff room

Head's office

TRY THIS!

Make a black-and-white copy of a map of your school. Colour rooms with different uses in different colours. You could add symbols to show activities such as gym, music and science that go on in different rooms.

SCHOOL GROUNDS IN A GRID

Have you ever noticed that many maps are divided into squares?

Lines running up and across the map form a grid, which you can use to locate places exactly.

Grid references

This map of a school grounds has a grid. The squares running across the page have letters. The squares running up the page have numbers. The letters and numbers pinpoint a particular square, such as B2. This is called a grid reference.

Grid references are always given in a certain order. Start at the bottom left corner of the map. Run your finger ALONG letters at the bottom, then UP the numbers.

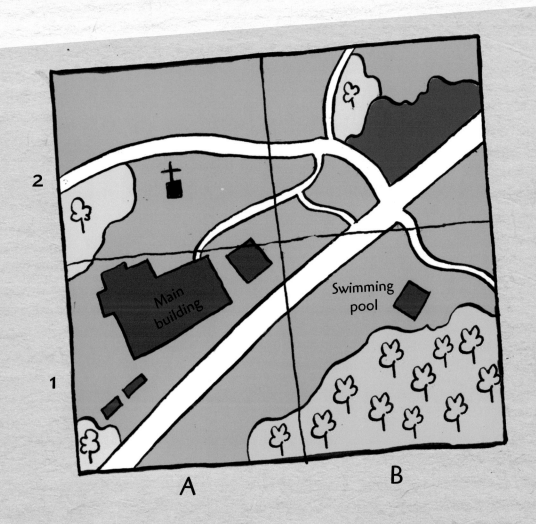

TRY THIS!

Look at the map and answer these questions:

- What feature can you see in square A2?
- Give the grid reference for the swimming pool.

MAP YOUR ROUTE TO SCHOOL

How do you get to school? Do you come on foot, or by bike or car? Whatever method you use, you can use a street map to trace your route.

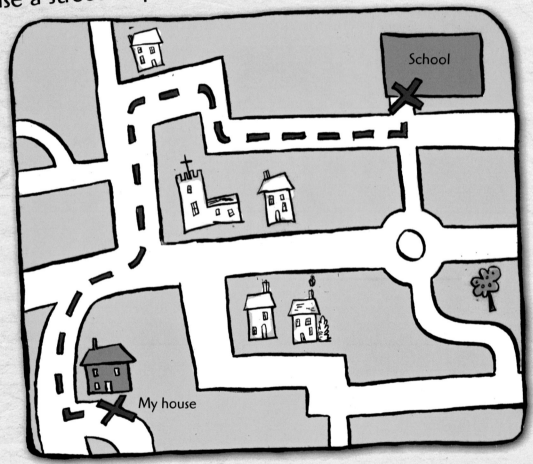

Street maps

Street maps are large-scale maps. They show a small area in a lot of detail, so they are useful for short journeys, or the last part of a long journey. These maps show the names of streets and other features that are useful for drivers, such as car parks.

TRY THIS!

Make a map of your own journey to school from memory. Mark any landmarks you pass on the way. When your map is complete, compare it with a local map. How accurate was your map?

GOING BY BUS

Many children get to school by bus. Bus journeys are shown on special street maps like the one below. The routes of several buses are shown in different colours.

Stops are marked so people know exactly where to get on and off.

KEY

◯ Bus stop

▬ 41 bus route

▬ 52 bus route

Elm Avenue

SCH

Sefton Street

Rose Hill

Oak St

Lea Dr

Essex Road

Clifton Road

Route maps

Some transport maps don't show the town or streets at all. Route maps like the one on the next page show only the stops on a route, and where bus routes connect. If you need to change buses on your way to school, these maps make it easy to plan your route.

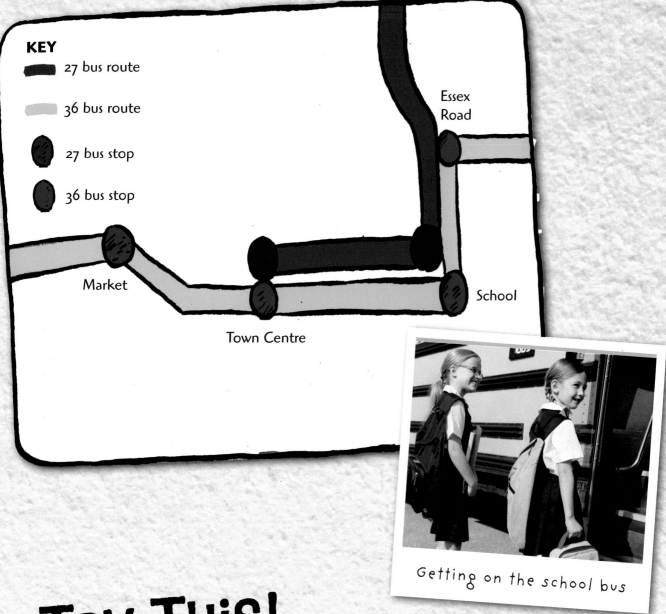

KEY

▬ 27 bus route

▬ 36 bus route

⬤ 27 bus stop

⬤ 36 bus stop

Essex Road

Market

Town Centre

School

Getting on the school bus

TRY THIS!

Look at the street map on the opposite page and and answer these questions:

- Name two buses that take you to school?
- What bus would you take to school if you lived on Rose Hill?

OUTING WITH A ROAD MAP

School's out! Your class is going on a school outing. If you are planning a long journey like this, you will need a road map.

These small-scale maps show a large area, so you can see the whole journey on a page.

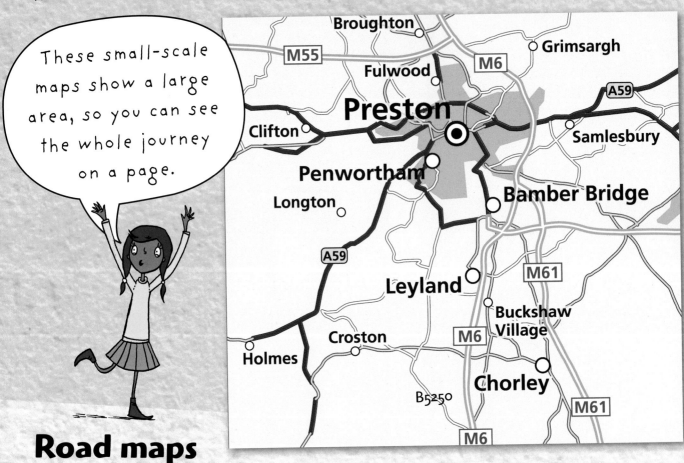

Road maps

Road maps don't show the landscape accurately. Towns and villages are shown as dots or coloured areas. Motorways, main roads and country lanes are shown as lines of different colours. Road numbers are shown on the map and also on road signs, so drivers can plan a route and find the way.

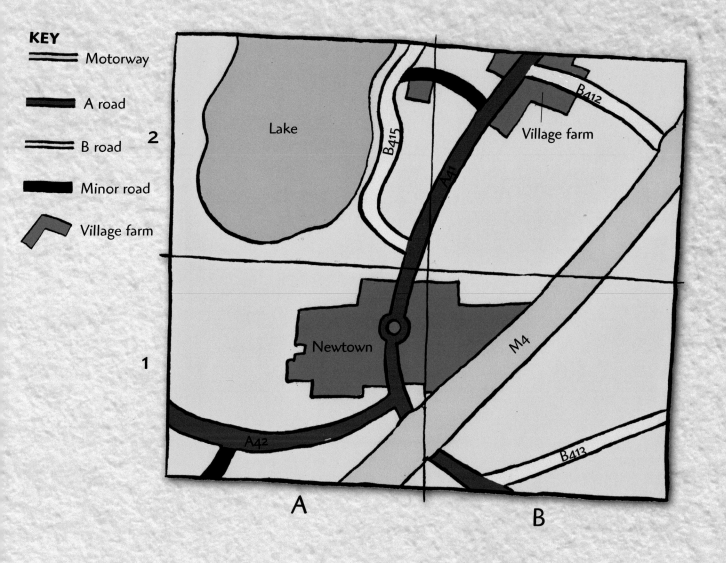

KEY

Motorway

A road

B road

Minor road

Village farm

TRY THIS!

Look at the map. The school bus is taking your class from Newtown in A1 to the lake in A2. On the way back you will visit the farm near the lake. Plan a round trip that goes one way and comes back a different way.

What the words mean

Accurate Of something that is correct or right.

Aerial view A view from above.

Architect A person who designs buildings

Compass A tool that shows directions and helps you find your way.

Compass rose A symbol that shows compass directions.

Grid Squares on a map made by lines running up, down and across the page.

Grid reference Directions provided by the grid on a map.

Land use map A map that shows what land or buildings are used for.

Locate To find.

Key A panel on a map that shows the meaning of symbols.

Plan A map that shows a small area, such as a building or room.

Road map A map of a large area that shows roads, and is useful on journeys.

Scale The size a map is drawn to.

Street map A map of a town or village that gives the names of streets.

Symbol A sign or picture that stands for something in real life.

More Information

Books

Jack Gillet and Meg Gillet, *Maps and Mapping Skills: Introducing Maps* (Wayland, 2014)

Sally Hewitt, *Project Geography: Maps* (Franklin Watts, 2013)

Claire Llewellyn, *Ways Into Geography: Using Maps* (Franklin Watts, 2012)

Websites

Mapskills (PowerPoint) – Think Geography

www.thinkgeography.org.uk/Year%20 8%20Geog/.../Mapskills.ppt
This site explains map skills and has lots of exercises to practise your map skills.

Ordnance Survey: Map reading made easy

http://mapzone ordnancesurvey co.uk/ mapzone/PagesHomeworkHelp/docs/ easypeasy.pdf
Download this handy guide to map reading.

BBC – GCSE Bitesize: Basics of mapping: 1

www.bbc.co.uk/schools/gcsebitesize/ geography/geographical_skills/maps_ rev1.shtml
A summary of map reading skills for pupils learning geography at school.

Index